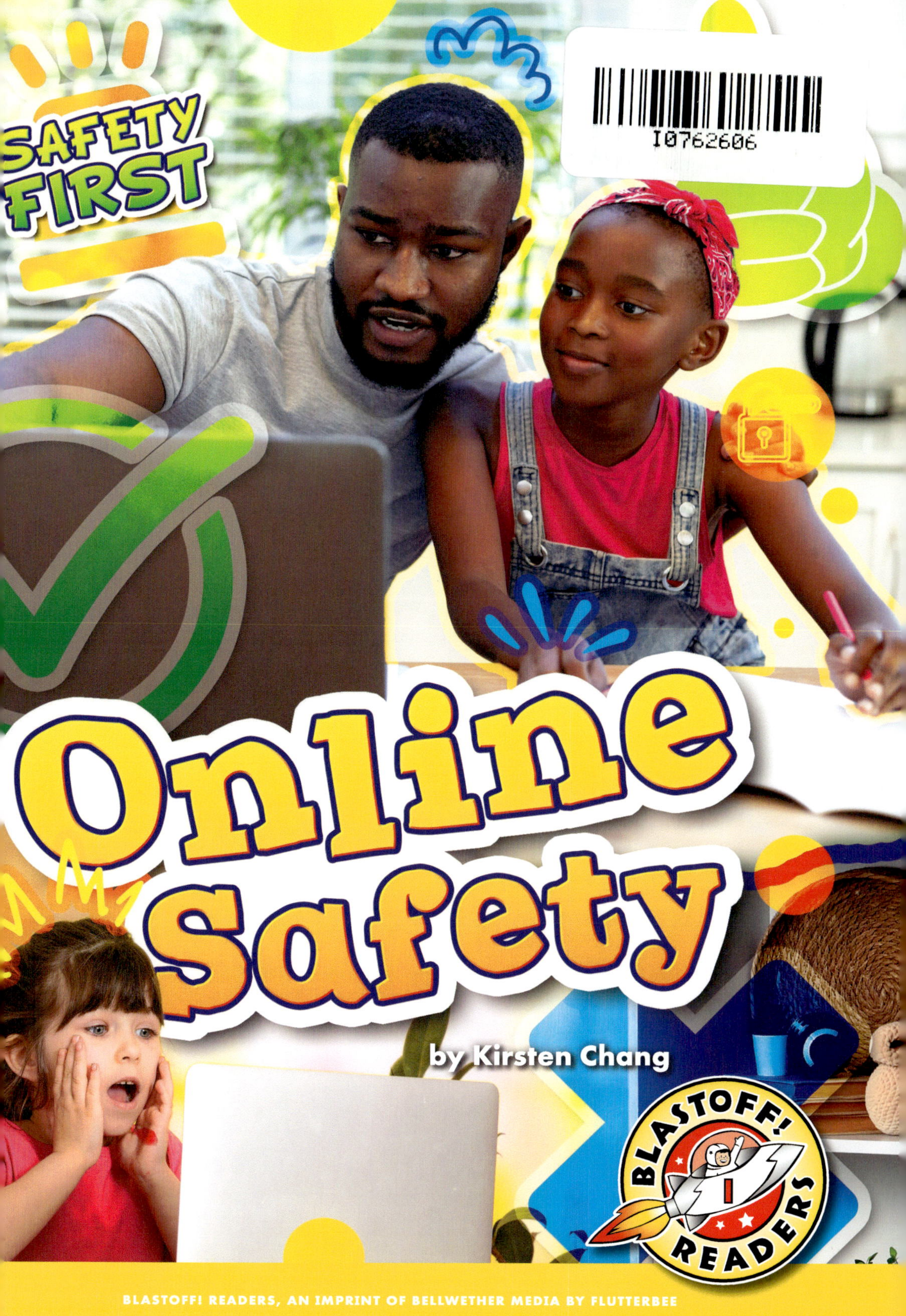

Online Safety

by Kirsten Chang

BLASTOFF! READERS, AN IMPRINT OF BELLWETHER MEDIA BY FLUTTERBEE

Blastoff! Readers are carefully developed by literacy experts to build reading stamina and move students toward fluency by combining standards-based content with developmentally appropriate text.

Level 1 provides the most support through repetition of high-frequency words, light text, predictable sentence patterns, and strong visual support.

Level 2 offers early readers a bit more challenge through varied sentences, increased text load, and text-supportive special features.

Level 3 advances early-fluent readers toward fluency through increased text load, less reliance on photos, advancing concepts, longer sentences, and more complex special features.

★ **Blastoff! Universe**

Reading Level

Grade K

Grades 1–3

Grade 4

This edition first published in 2027 by Bellwether Media, Inc.

For information regarding permission, write to Bellwether Media, Inc., Attention: Permissions Department, 3500 American Blvd W, Suite 150, Bloomington, MN 55431.

Library of Congress Cataloging-in-Publication Data is available at www.loc.gov or upon request from the publisher.

ISBN: 9798898800376 (hardcover)
ISBN: 9798898802905 (paperback)
ISBN: 9798898801618 (ebook)

Editor: Rachael Barnes Designer: Andrea Schneider

Printed in the United States of America, North Mankato, MN.

Table of Contents

Gaming Safely

Ian plays games
on his tablet.
He follows rules
to stay safe online!

tablet

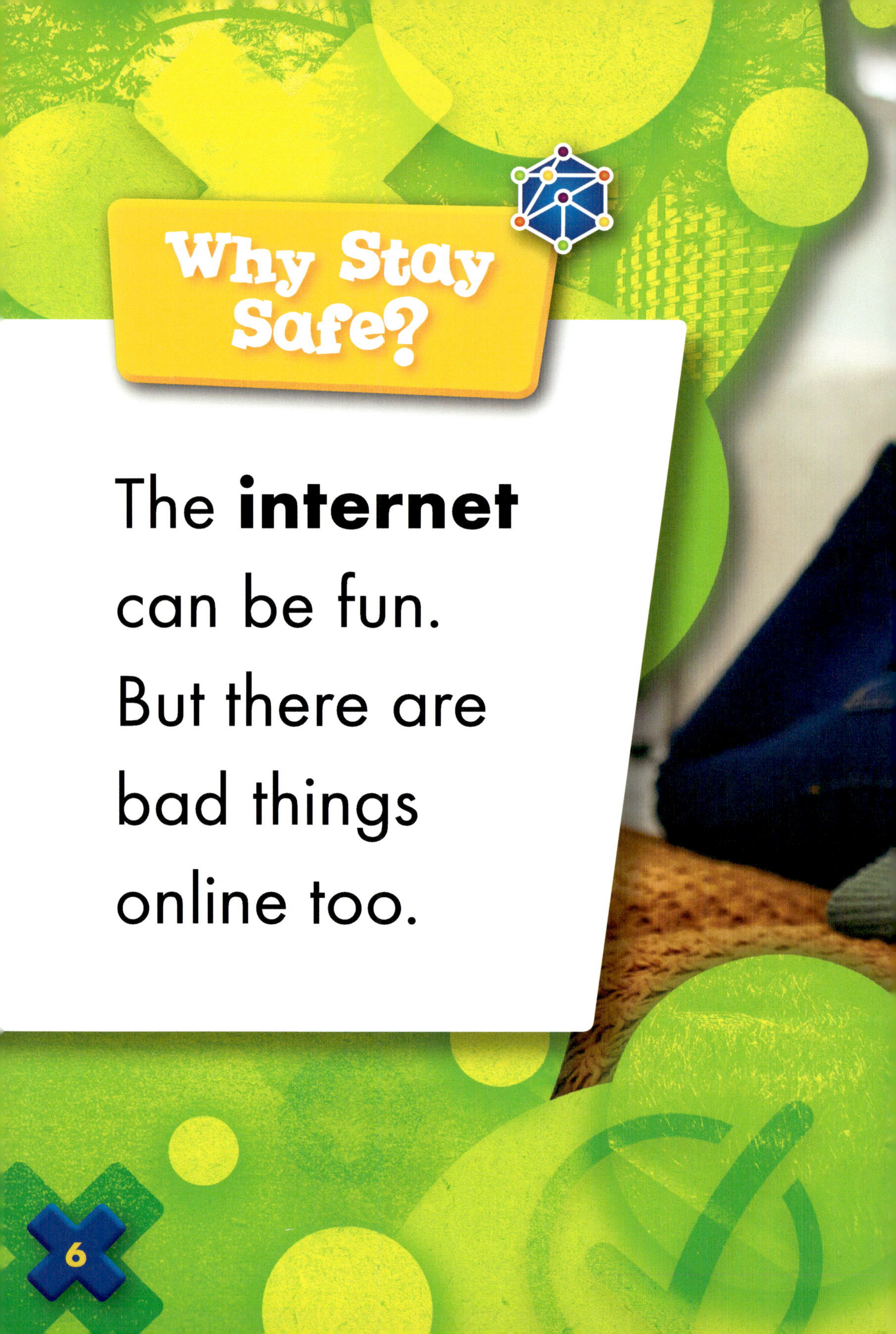

Why Stay Safe?

The **internet** can be fun. But there are bad things online too.

Strangers can take **information** from others online. We keep our information **private**.

People online can be mean. We tell a trusted adult about **bullying**.

bullying

Staying Safe

Grace watches funny videos. Mom watches too. She makes sure the videos are for kids!

Eli plays a video game. He only plays with friends he meets in person.

Lucy makes a strong **password**. She does not share it with strangers.

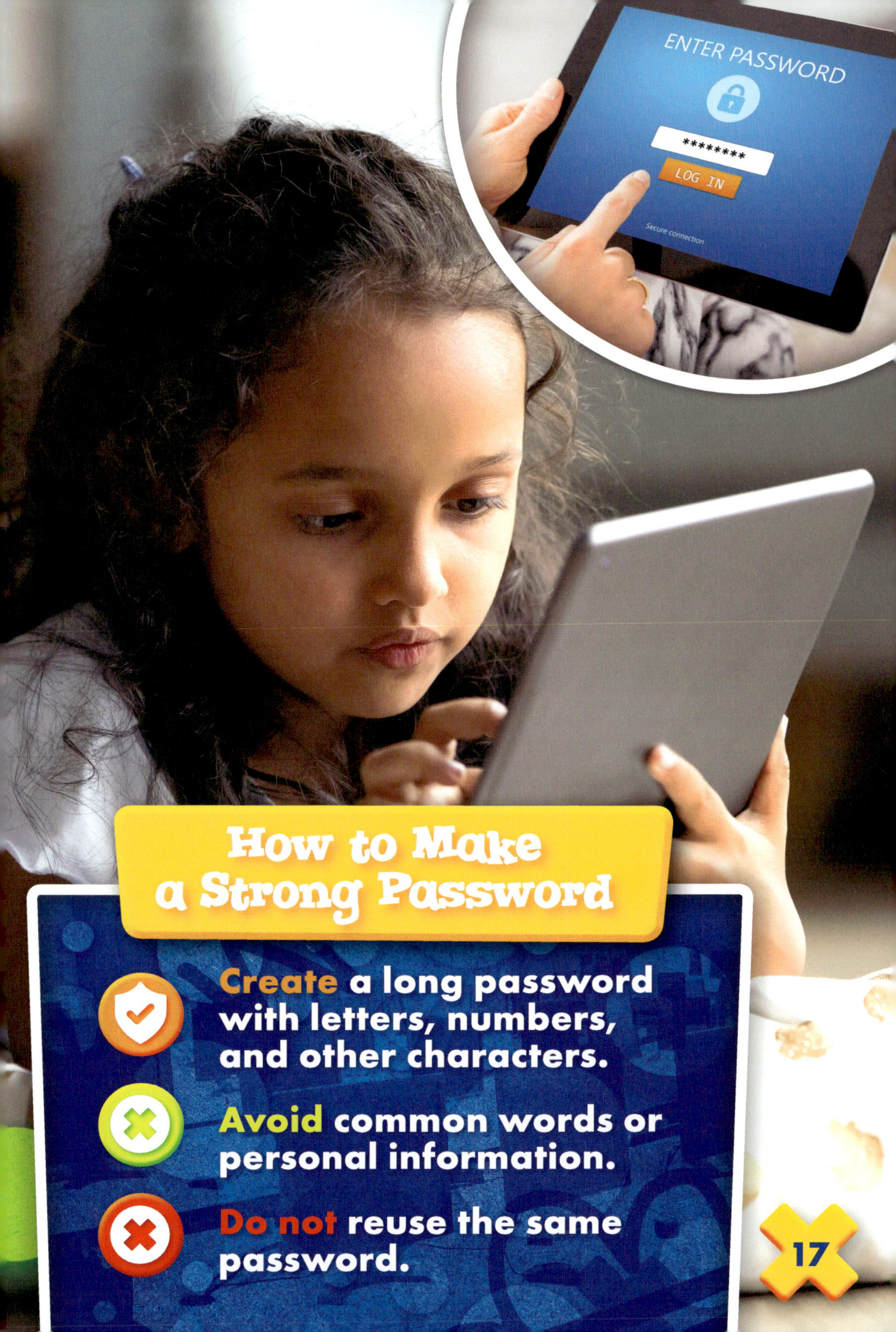

How to Make a Strong Password

- **Create** a long password with letters, numbers, and other characters.
- **Avoid** common words or personal information.
- **Do not** reuse the same password.

Dylan wants a new **app**. He asks Dad before he gets it.

apps

Cora's screen time is over. She goes outside to play!

Safety Rules
Only talk to friends you know in real life.
Do not share information about yourself with strangers.
Ask before buying anything online.
Balance screen time with other kinds of play.

Glossary

app

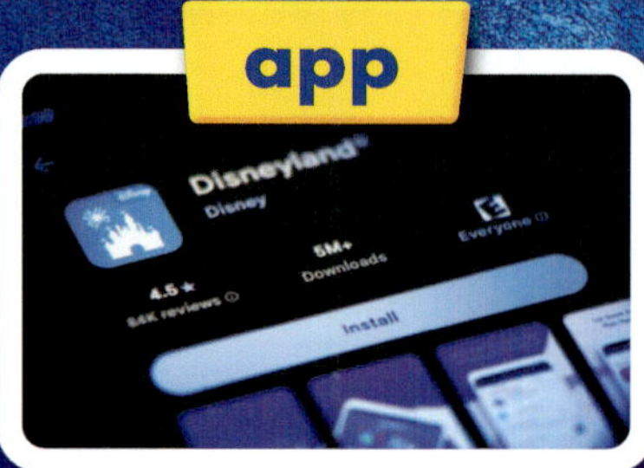

a program for a cell phone or other mobile device

bullying

unwanted, hurtful behavior online or in person that is often repeated

information

facts and knowledge

internet

a system of computers that allows people around the world to talk to one another

password

a secret code required to get into personal things online

private

not meant for other people to know about

To Learn More

AT THE LIBRARY

Clark, Katie. *Using Mobile Devices*. Minneapolis, Minn.: Lerner Publications, 2026.

Heos, Bridget. *Be Safe on the Internet*. Mankato, Minn.: Amicus, 2026.

Owens, Layla. *I Stay Safe*. Buffalo, N.Y.: Enslow Publishing, 2026.

ON THE WEB

FACTSURFER

Factsurfer.com gives you a safe, fun way to find more information.

1. Go to www.factsurfer.com.
2. Enter "online safety" into the search box and click 🔍.
3. Select your book cover to see a list of related content.

Index

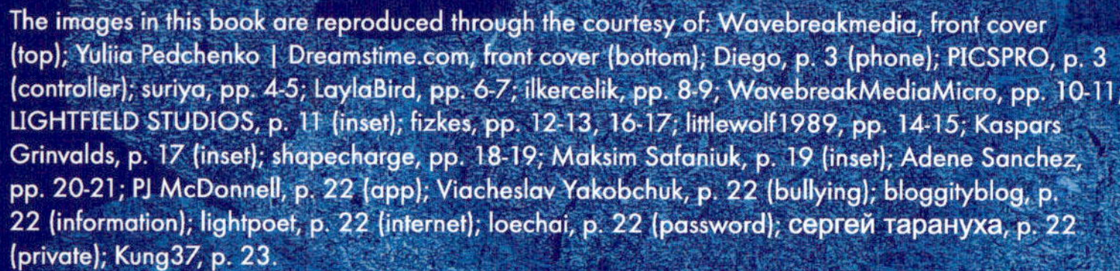

The images in this book are reproduced through the courtesy of: Wavebreakmedia, front cover (top); Yuliia Pedchenko | Dreamstime.com, front cover (bottom); Diego, p. 3 (phone); PICSPRO, p. 3 (controller); suriya, pp. 4-5; LaylaBird, pp. 6-7; ilkercelik, pp. 8-9; WavebreakMediaMicro, pp. 10-11; LIGHTFIELD STUDIOS, p. 11 (inset); fizkes, pp. 12-13, 16-17; littlewolf1989, pp. 14-15; Kaspars Grinvalds, p. 17 (inset); shapecharge, pp. 18-19; Maksim Safaniuk, p. 19 (inset); Adene Sanchez, pp. 20-21; PJ McDonnell, p. 22 (app); Viacheslav Yakobchuk, p. 22 (bullying); bloggityblog, p. 22 (information); lightpoet, p. 22 (internet); loechai, p. 22 (password); сергей тарануха, p. 22 (private); Kung37, p. 23.